Juan Riochí Siafá

MINIMALISM
A philosophy that will transform your personal and financial life

Author of the text: Juan Riochí Siafá
Title: MINIMALISM. A philosophy that will transform your personal
and financial life
Edition: June 2023

Copyright © 2023 Juan Riochí Siafá
juanriochi@gmail.com

Services for editing and publication:
BooKyAM. Editorial Services for publication on Amazon
www.bookyam.com bookyam.info@gmail.com

Interior and cover layout: Click Layout www.clicmaquetacion.com
clic.maquetacion@gmail.com

ISBN: See back cover barcode
Editorial Seal: Independent publication of the author himself (PI)
Personal Improvement. S.L

Do not dream about the things you do not have; rather recognize the blessings of the things you do have. Then, remember gratefully how anxious you would be if your possessions weren't yours.

MARCUS AURELIUS
(Meditations)

Index

Introduction

In the fast-paced, consumerist world we live in, many individuals have found a yearning for a more meaningful and balanced life. In this context, minimalism has gained popularity as a philosophy of life that promotes simplicity, clarity, and intentionality in all aspects of our existence.

Minimalism is much more than just a passing trend; It is a movement that is transforming the way people approach their lives, homes, relationships and values. As we face a growing avalanche of distractions and demands, minimalism invites us to reconsider our priorities and shed everything superfluous, to focus on what really matters.

In this book, we will explore in detail the rise of minimalism today, its foundations, and how it has managed to resonate in modern society. Through practical tips, we will discover how minimalism can improve our quality of life and allow us to find true happiness in a world full of possibilities.

First, we will dive into the fundamental principles of minimalism, unraveling its philosophical roots and exploring how it has adapted to the challenges of the twenty-first century. We will analyze how minimalism goes beyond the simple reduction of material belongings and extends to our way of thinking, our relationships and our personal goals.

Next, we will delve into the impact of minimalism on different aspects of our lives. From organizing our home to managing time and taking care of our mental health, we'll discover how the minimalist approach can help us simplify and optimize each area.

In addition, we will explore the role of minimalism in sustainability and environmental preservation. In a world concerned about climate change and the overexploitation of resources, minimalism is presented as a conscious and responsible alternative, encouraging the reduction of consumption and the production of waste.

Finally, we will examine how minimalism has influenced art, fashion, architecture and other cultural manifestations. We will see how minimalist design has become a cherished aesthetic and how artists and creators are using this philosophy as a form of expression and social critique.

Throughout this journey, we'll discover that minimalism goes beyond simply getting rid of things; It's about clearing our minds, setting clear priorities, and living with intention. In an increasingly chaotic world, minimalism offers us an avenue to find peace, balance, and meaning in our lives.

Get ready to embark on this journey to a simpler and more meaningful life!

Chapter 1

General aspects of minimalist philosophy

Minimalism is an artistic movement and lifestyle that is characterized by simplicity, reduction of elements and elimination of the superfluous. It emerged in the twentieth century, mainly in the visual arts, but subsequently expanded into other areas, including architecture, design, music and lifestyle.

Its origin as an artistic movement can be traced back to the 1960s in the United States. It was a reaction against the abstract expressionism and pop art that were prevalent at the time. Minimalist artists sought to move away from the subjectivity and emotional content of art, focusing on simple geometric shapes, neutral colors, and the removal of any non-essential elements. Some of the most prominent artists associated with minimalism include Donald Judd, Dan Flavin, Carl Andre, and Agnes Martin.

As minimalism spread to other areas beyond art, it also became a lifestyle and philosophy. Today, minimalism is applied in various forms. Some people adopt a minimalist lifestyle by reducing the amount of material possessions, focusing on the essentials, and eliminating physical and mental clutter. This means living with fewer things, shopping more mindfully, and simplifying daily routines.

Minimalism has also extended to interior design and architecture, where simplicity, functionality and clean aesthetics are sought. Clean lines, neutral colors and open spaces are used to create serene and uncluttered environments.

In the digital realm, minimalism is reflected in the design of interfaces and websites, where white spaces, simple typography and intuitive navigation are privileged.

The application of minimalism today can help counter rampant consumerism, promote sustainability, and foster a more conscious and balanced approach to life. By simplifying our lives, we can free up time and energy to focus on what really matters to us, such as personal relationships, personal growth, and the pursuit of happiness and fulfillment through meaningful experiences rather than the accumulation of material goods.

Minimalism has a close relationship with Zen philosophy and yoga, and there are connections and commonalities between these three approaches. It shares a mindset like Zen philosophy, which is based on simplicity, mindfulness, and appreciation of things as they are. Both minimalism and Zen emphasize the importance of reducing desire and attaching oneself to material possessions, recognizing that true happiness and satisfaction do not come from the accumulation of goods, but from the appreciation of what we already have in the present moment.

Yoga, on the other hand, can also relate to minimalism. Yoga is a physical, mental and spiritual practice that seeks union and balance between body and mind. As people engage in the practice of yoga, they often become more aware of their body, their needs, and their environment. This can lead to a more conscious and simplified approach to life, where excess is sought to be eliminated, both in terms of material possessions and unnecessary thoughts and emotions.

In addition, yoga promotes detachment and non-identification with the ego, which is aligned with the principles of minimalism. Both philosophies emphasize the importance of living in the present, cultivating gratitude, and finding fulfillment in life's simple experiences.

Minimalism also has a close relationship with philosophy in several aspects. Although minimalism originated primarily as an art movement and lifestyle, it also has profound philosophical implications. Here are some ways minimalism relates to philosophy:

- Simplicity and essence: Minimalism seek simplicity and reduction to the essential. This idea is related to the philosophy of minimalism in which it questions what is essential in life and seeks to eliminate the superfluous. This is in line with philosophical philosophy that examines the essence of things and seeks to find truth and clarity through simplification.

- Ethics and consumption: Minimalism can also have an ethical and critical dimension towards unbridled consumerism. In this sense, it relates to moral and ethical philosophy, where we reflect on how our choices and actions impact ourselves, others, and the world at large. Minimalism can advocate for more conscious and sustainable consumption, and this is based on ethical and philosophical considerations about our lifestyle and our responsibilities towards the environment.

- Existentialism: Minimalism also has ties to existentialism, a philosophical current that examines human existence and the search for meaning. Minimalism can raise questions about life's purpose, authenticity, and liberation from unnecessary burdens. By focusing on the essential, minimalism can open space for reflection and exploration of one's existence.

- Eastern philosophy: As I mentioned earlier, minimalism shares connections with Zen philosophy and yoga. These Eastern philosophical traditions focus on mindfulness, simplicity, and connection to the present moment. Minimalism adopts elements of these Eastern philosophies and integrates them into its approach to life and aesthetic style.

In the context of minimalist philosophy, it is important to note that minimalism does not have a specific group of authors or promoters in the strict sense of a formal philosophical current. However, there are thinkers, philosophers and writers who have addressed issues related to simplicity, essence and reduction in their works. Here are some prominent names:

- Epicurus: Epicurus was an ancient Greek philosopher who promoted a philosophy centered on the pursuit of happiness and pleasure through simplicity and moderation. In his school, known as the Garden, ataraxia (tranquility) was valued and emphasis was placed on the elimination of unnecessary desires.

- Henry David Thoreau: Thoreau was an American writer and philosopher known for his work "Walden", in which he narrates his experience living in nature in a simple and autonomous way. Thoreau advocated life in harmony with nature and the search for the essence of existence.

- Diogenes of Sinope: Diogenes was a Cynic philosopher of ancient Greece who lived extremely simply and rejected luxuries and social conventions. His philosophy was towards autarky and living in conformity with nature.

- Zen Buddhism: Although there are no specific authors in Zen Buddhism, this philosophical and spiritual tradition has influenced minimalist philosophy. Zen promotes mindfulness, simplicity, and appreciation of the present moment, and has had a significant impact on the conception and practice of minimalism.

While these names do not represent an exhaustive list, they are examples of thinkers whose ideas and approaches are related to the principles of minima-

lism and have influenced the conception and development of this philosophy of life. It is important to
note that minimalism is not limited solely to philosophy but is also expressed in other disciplines such as
art, design and lifestyle.

In short, minimalism can be considered as a philosophical response to the challenges and demands
of modern life. It seeks a more meaningful and
conscious way of life and draws on various philosophical currents to base its principles and values.

Chapter 2

Sustainability and preservation of the environment

In a world increasingly aware of environmental challenges, minimalism emerges as a philosophical and lifestyle approach that can play an important role in sustainability and environmental preservation. In this chapter, we will explore how the principles of minimalism, such as reducing consumption and simplifying needs, can contribute to environmental protection, foster sustainability, and promote a lifestyle that is more respectful of natural resources.

One of the fundamental principles of this movement is conscious consumption. Minimalism invites us to reflect on our real needs and avoid excessive and unbridled consumption. By reducing our impulse purchases and considering the durability and environmental impact of the products we purchase, we can decrease waste and reduce our ecological footprint.

It promotes the simplification of our lives and our spaces. By getting rid of unnecessary objects and keeping only the essentials, we reduce the number of resources we consume and decrease the amount of waste we generate. In addition, living in simpler, clearer spaces helps us appreciate what we have and find fulfillment in experiences and relationships, rather than accumulating material possessions.

Value quality over quantity. Instead of having multiple low-quality objects that wear out quickly, minimalism encourages us to invest in durable, high-quality products. This not only reduces the need to constantly replace our objects, but also prevents excessive production and waste generation.

Minimalism aligns with the principles of the circular economy, which seeks to maximize the use of resources and minimize waste. By opting for reuse, recycling and exchange of goods, minimalism encourages the reduction of the extraction of raw materials and the production of new products, thus contributing to a more sustainable and circular approach to the economy.

It can also encourage environmental awareness and activism. By adopting a minimalist lifestyle, we become more aware of the interconnections between our actions and the environment. This can motivate us to participate in movements and actions that promote sustainability, such as climate activism, advocating for biodiversity conservation, and promoting renewable energy.

In short, it is a lifestyle that offers a valuable approach to addressing today's environmental challenges. Through conscious consumption, the simplification of life and space, the focus on quality and durability we will achieve a more sustainable, balanced and adjusted economy to everyone.

Chapter 3

Living a Life with Purpose and Fulfillment

Minimalism has several benefits and can have a significant impact on our lives such as clarity and focus, stress reduction, freedom and flexibility, sustainability and respect for the environment and finally meaningful connections and relationships.

The minimalist lifestyle helps us focus on what really matters in our lives. By simplifying our possessions, our routines, and our goals, we can eliminate clutter and unnecessary distractions, allowing us to have greater mental clarity and focus on what's important to us. At the same time, you can reduce stress by eliminating excess worries and responsibilities. By simplifying our lives, we can free ourselves from the burden of maintaining and organizing an excess of material possessions. In addition, by getting rid of the superfluous, we can also reduce financial stress by spending less and living more sustainably.

It gives us greater freedom and flexibility. By owning fewer things and being less attached to them, we can be more mobile and open to new opportunities. We can also have more financial freedom by reducing unnecessary expenses and being able to invest in what we really value.

It also promotes a more conscious and responsible consumption. By reducing the number of things, we buy and own, we reduce our environmental impact and contribute to a more sustainable lifestyle. Minimalism encourages reuse, recycling and support for ethical and environmentally friendly products and companies.

By simplifying our lives, we can devote more time and energy to cultivating meaningful relationships. By having fewer distractions and commitments, we can be more present and engaged in our personal relationships, which strengthens emotional bonds and gives us a greater sense of connection and belonging. Each person can adapt minimalism to their lifestyle and define what is important to themselves, with the aim of living more consciously, balanced and authentically.

We often feel that our lives are a mess and that there is no room for order; that our existence is trapped in what we call "mouse roulette" or the circle of consumerism. However, we can transform our lives with the simple effort of understanding the difference between "NEEDING" and "WANTING" something and opening a dialogue in the depths of our SELF.

Most of the things we buy we do from the approach of "WANT" and months later we realize that we do not really need them in our lives. It has happened to all of us that we buy a few pairs of new shoes, a dress or a shirt and forget about them for months, sometimes years, with the label on. Acting in this way does not indicate that we are rare beings from another planet and that we do not fit into society. Well, I must tell you that today's society is designed for us to act in this way, that is, to consume unbridled ruin our lives and financial expectations.

We must be aware and know that impulsive consumption is a common and widely promoted phenomenon in our society. Advertising, marketing and easy access to products and services through online platforms all contribute to encouraging impulsive consumption. Advertising is designed to generate wants and needs in consumers. Use persuasive techniques, such as emotional messages, irresistible promotions, and creating a sense of scarcity or urgency, to drive impulse buying.

On the other hand, technology and e-commerce have facilitated access to a wide range of products and services. The ability to make purchases with a single click and receive the products in a short time encourages impulsive consumption, since gratification is instantaneous. In the same way, the environment and social networks can also influence impulsive consumption. The pressure to keep up with the latest trends and the desire to be socially accepted can lead people to buy things they don't really need, as our current society tends to value the accumulation of material goods as a sign of success and happiness. This creates a "more is better" mentality, leading to excessive and impulsive consumption to satisfy that constant search for more things. In short, impulsive consumption can have negative consequences, both at the individual level and at the social and environmental level. It can lead to financial problems, debt accumulation, stress, dissatisfaction and waste of resources.

To counteract impulsive consumption, it's important to develop a more mindful and thoughtful approach to shopping such as taking a moment to assess whether you really need the product or if it's a momentary boost. Ask yourself if the product fits with your long-term values and goals.

In the same way, defining a budget will help you be more aware of your expenses and avoid impulse purchases that do not fit your financial possibilities.

If you feel the urge to buy something, take some time to think about it and consider whether you really need it. Often, by waiting for a period, the desire to buy fades.

And like a good minimalist, consider living with less and focusing on what's important to you. As we have highlighted in previous paragraphs, minimalism promotes simplicity, the reduction of consumption and the focus on meaningful experiences and relationships rather than material possessions. Ultimately, it's about being aware of your consumption choices and making informed decisions aligned with your real values and needs.

We will conclude this chapter by emphasizing the difference between "WANT" and "NEED." "WANT" and "NEED" relate to our basic motivations and requirements. When we want something, it is a desire or longing to possess, experience or achieve something. Desires are often influenced by emotional, social, and cultural factors. "WANTING" something implies that we would like to have it, but it is not necessarily essential to our survival or basic well-being.

For example, wanting a new mobile phone, a luxury car or a pair of fashionable shoes are desires that are driven by our tastes, preferences and the influence of society. On the other hand, a "NEED" refers to something that is fundamental to our survival, well-being, or proper functioning. Necessities are essential elements that we require to live a healthy, safe and fulfilling life. Examples of basic needs include food, water, shelter, clothing, access to health care, education, and meaningful social relationships.

It is important to differentiate between "WANT" and "NEED" to make more conscious decisions in our lives. Often, we mistake our desires for needs and end up chasing things that are not essential to our true happiness and well-being.

By practicing reflection and clarity about our real needs, we can focus our resources and efforts on satisfying the essentials and avoid falling into impulsive and excessive consumption. This can lead to greater satisfaction and balance in our lives, aligning our actions with what we really need for our physical, emotional and spiritual well-being.

Chapter 4

Simplifying and Harmonizing Spaces

Minimalism can have a significant effect on the home, transforming the physical and emotional environment. Here are some of the positive effects minimalism can have on your home:

- Clear space: By taking a minimalist approach, you get rid of excess possessions and keep only what you really need and value. This creates a more spacious and uncluttered environment in your home, which can lead to a sense of calm and tranquility.

- Less clutter: Minimalism involves getting rid of unnecessary clutter. By having fewer objects in your home, there are fewer things to organize, clean and maintain. This saves you time and energy and reduces the feeling of being overwhelmed by household responsibilities.

- Ease of organization: With fewer possessions, it's easier to keep your home organized. Each object has its designated place and there is no accumulation of things that hinder the organization. This allows you to find things more easily and avoids the feeling of constantly searching or losing objects.

- Greater attention to quality: By embracing minimalism, you tend to value quality over quantity more. You opt for durable, functional, high-quality objects instead of accumulating low-quality or temporary-use objects. This can lead to an improvement in the aesthetics and functionality of your home.

- Increased focus on aesthetics: Minimalism is often associated with a clean, simple and elegant design. By eliminating distractions and visual clutter, an aesthetically pleasing and harmonious environment is created. This can generate a sense of peace and well-being when entering your home.

- Reduced emotional load: It can also have an emotional effect on your home. By freeing yourself from unnecessary possessions, you get rid of objects that may be associated with emotional burdens or unwanted memories. This can generate a sense of release and facilitate the flow of positive energy in your home.

Remember that minimalism is a personal approach and can be adapted according to your own needs and preferences. Each person may experience the effects of minimalism differently, but overall, it can help you create a more tidy, serene, and welcoming home.

Minimalism can at the same time have a significant impact on the economy of the family home. Here are some aspects that you can positively influence:

- Saving money: You tend to reduce your expenses and spend less on impulse and unnecessary purchases. By being more aware of your consumption choices, you can avoid buying things that are not essential and focus your financial resources on what really matters. This can lead to long-term money savings.

- More conscious shopping: Promotes conscious and thoughtful shopping. Before making a purchase, you ask yourself if you really need the product and if it has lasting value. This can help you avoid impulse purchases and choose quality products that are durable and functional, rather than low-quality products that would have to be replaced frequently.

- Debt reduction: By reducing your expenses and avoiding unnecessary purchases, you can have more control over your finances and reduce your debts. Minimalism encourages living within your means and avoiding the accumulation of unnecessary debt, which can lead to greater financial stability for your home.

- Less maintenance costs: By having fewer possessions and a clearer home, there are fewer things that need maintenance and care. This can lead to decreased costs associated with maintaining your home, such as repairs, cleaning, and storage.

- Greater focus on experiences: Tends to focus on experiences and relationships rather than material possessions. Instead of spending money hoarding things, you can invest it in meaningful experiences for you and your family, such as travel, joint activities, or education. This can lead to greater satisfaction and enrichment in family life.

- Lower environmental impact: It can also contribute to a more sustainable and environmentally conscious economy. By reducing your consumption and choosing quality, durable and sustainable products, you are supporting environmentally responsible practices. This can help reduce your ecological footprint and contribute to protecting the environment for future generations.

Minimalism has a close relationship with the space in the home, as it promotes the idea of having a clear, functional and harmonious space. Here are some key aspects of how it relates to space in the home:

- Clear clutter: It involves getting rid of excess possessions and keeping only what is necessary and valued. This involves removing unnecessary clutter and creating a more orderly and uncluttered physical space. By having fewer objects, there is more space available in your home, which generates a feeling of spaciousness and calm.

- Efficient use of space: Encourages the efficient use of space in the home. By reducing possessions and keeping only the essentials, you can maximize the use of every area of your home. This means having multifunctional furniture and objects, as well as using smart storage solutions that make the most of every available corner.

- Greater sense of spaciousness: By eliminating excess furniture, decorations and objects, your home can look more spacious and spacious. This creates a sense of freedom and lightness in the environment, which can contribute to greater comfort and well-being in your home.

- Focus on quality over quantity: This involves investing in durable and functional furniture, as well as decorative elements and accessories that really bring aesthetic value and utility. By opting for quality instead of quantity, you can reduce the number of objects in your home and have a more orderly and aesthetically pleasing space.

- Visual harmony: Look for visual harmony in the home. By having a clear space and a careful selection of objects, a sense of balance and fluidity is created in the decoration and arrangement of the elements in the home. This can contribute to a sense of visual peace and tranquility.

- Flexibility and adaptability: It allow you to have a more flexible and adaptable space to your changing needs. By having fewer objects and a focus on functionality, you can rearrange and adapt your home to your specific requirements at different times in your life.

Finally, minimalism can have a significant impact on family relationships within the home such as:

- Increased quality time together: You tend to focus on what really matters, like spending quality time with your family. By reducing excess possessions and distractions, you can devote more time and attention to your loved ones. This fosters greater emotional connection, strengthens family bonds, and creates meaningful shared memories.

- Less stress and tensions: Minimalism can help reduce stress and tensions in the home. By having a clearer and more orderly space, there is less disorder and chaos that can lead to conflicts and family tensions. In addition, by focusing on the essentials and simplifying your lifestyle, you can reduce the burden of responsibilities and demands, which contributes to a more relaxed and harmonious atmosphere at home.

- Encouraging communication and collaboration: By having fewer distractions and material possessions, minimalism can promote open communication and collaboration at home. By being less focused on things, you can pay more attention to the needs and opinions of other family members. This facilitates more effective communication and greater collaboration on household chores, promoting a sense of teamwork and mutual support.

- Focus on shared experiences: Tends to value experiences more than material possessions. By focusing on living more intentionally, you can plan shared activities and experiences instead of hoarding things. This promotes moments of fun, adventure and family learning, which strengthens family bonds and creates lasting memories.

- Teaching values and responsibility: It can be an opportunity to teach family members about the value of things, conscious consumption and responsibility. Having fewer possessions fosters a mindset of caring and appreciation for what you have. In addition, minimalism can help instill habits of organization, order, and responsibility in all family members.

• Stimulation of creativity and imagination: By having fewer toys and material distractions, children can learn to stimulate their creativity and use their imagination more actively. This promotes free play, exploration and the development of creative skills. In addition, simplifying the environment can inspire the family to seek creative activities and new ways to enjoy time together.

It's important to note that every family is unique, and the impact of minimalism can vary. The important thing is to adapt it to your own needs and family values, focusing on creating an environment that promotes connection, communication and shared happiness within the home.

Chapter 5

Simplifying and Cultivating a Healthy Relationship with Food

As we have highlighted before, minimalism is a lifestyle that is based on simplifying and minimizing possessions and activities to focus on the essentials. If we apply minimalism to our way of eating, it can be understood as looking for a simple diet, without excesses and focused on natural and nutritious foods. For this we must keep in mind the following aspects:

- Less is more: Instead of being overwhelmed with a wide variety of foods, we can choose to simplify our meals. This means choosing basic, nutritious ingredients instead of processed, additive-heavy foods. By reducing the number of options, it can also be easier to plan and prepare healthy meals.

- Basic and quality ingredients: It's about focusing on quality rather than quantity. We can apply this to our diet by opting for basic and quality ingredients. For example, choosing fresh and seasonal foods, whole grains, lean proteins, and healthy fats.

- Avoid food waste: It is of utmost importance to avoid waste. We can apply this principle in our way of eating by avoiding overbuying and using the foods we already have before buying more. Planning meals and properly storing food can help reduce food waste and save money.

- Simple cooking: Opting for simple recipes and preparations can be part of a minimalist diet. Instead of complicated culinary preparations, we can enjoy simple dishes that highlight the natural flavors of the ingredients. In addition, this can also save time and energy in the kitchen.

- Food awareness: Food awareness is also of utmost importance. By simplifying the way, we eat, we can be more present and aware of what we eat. This involves paying attention to our bodies, listening to our hunger and satiety cues, and fully enjoying distraction-free meals.

This way of acting can have a significant impact on our personal finances as, for example, cooking and eating at home instead of eating out is generally cheaper. By preparing our own meals, we can control ingredients, portions, and costs. In addition, eating at home reduces expenses associated with eating out, such as tips, taxes, and additional surcharges.

It also helps us plan meals. By planning our meals in advance, we can avoid unnecessary purchases and food waste. Planning allows us to create an accurate shopping list and buy only what we need. We can also take advantage of offers and discounts when making bulk purchases or taking advantage of sales of fresh seasonal foods, that is, buying staples. And, by focusing on basic, nutritious foods, we can save money compared to buying processed and packaged foods. Fresh foods, such as fruits, vegetables, whole grains, legumes, and lean proteins, tend to be both cheaper and healthier. In addition, these foods can be versatile and used in multiple recipes and motivate us to avoid unnecessary foods, since, by being aware of our purchases and food choices, we can avoid unnecessary food expenses. This includes unhealthy snacks, sugary drinks, processed foods, and expensive brand-name products. By focusing on basic and nutritious foods, we can maintain a tighter food budget.

Many people today are choosing to grow their own food. Growing our own food can be an excellent alternative today for several reasons:

- Food security: Growing our own food gives us greater food security. Instead of relying entirely on supermarkets and the supply chain, we can grow a portion of our food and have a more stable and reliable supply.

- Quality and freshness: When growing our own food, we have control over growing methods and can opt for organic and sustainable practices. This allows us to obtain fresher, higher quality food, without pesticides or other chemicals.

- Economic savings: Growing our own food can be a way to save money in the long run. While there may be upfront costs involved in installing the garden, the savings on long-term food purchase can be significant.

- Connecting with nature: Growing our own food connects us to nature and gives us a sense of satisfaction and gratification. It's a way to get actively involved in the cycle of life, learn about growing food, and appreciate the importance of land and natural resources.

- Reducing the ecological footprint: By growing our own food, we reduce the need for transportation and packaging of the food we buy in supermarkets. This helps reduce our ecological footprint and contributes to a more sustainable lifestyle.

However, it is important to note that growing our own food requires time, effort and basic gardening knowledge. Not everyone has access to adequate space to grow crops or the time needed to maintain a vegetable garden. In these cases, alternatives such as participation in community gardens or the purchase of food from local producers can also be explored. Growing our own food can be a rewarding and beneficial option, but each person must evaluate their situation and decide if it is a viable and suitable alternative for them.

We will conclude this chapter by offering some strategies on how to preserve food from the point of view of minimalist philosophy.

Minimalists typically adopt simple and efficient approaches to preserving food such as basic storage, freezing, dehydration, canning and pickling, and stock rotation. They often opt for basic and functional storage systems. They use simple containers and packaging, preferably reusable and without too many accessories or ornaments. This helps maintain a tidy and clutter-free storage space.

Another form of preservation is freezing, as it is a great way to preserve food in the long term. It is recommended to use efficient freezers in terms of space and energy. They organize food in labeled containers or freezer bags to prevent waste and make it easier to identify.

It is also common to use the method of dehydration to preserve food. They can use compact, easy-to-store food dehydrators to dry fruits, vegetables, and herbs. Dehydrated foods take up less space and keep well for long periods. Some minimalists practice preserving food using methods such as canning, pickling, or fermentation. These methods make it possible to extend the shelf life of food without taking up too much space in the refrigerator or freezer.

Finally, we have stock rotation which consists of following the philosophy of "first in, first out" to prevent food from spoiling. By rotating foods and consuming those that have a closer expiration date first, they can avoid waste and ensure that they use foods before they lose their freshness.

In short, people who practice minimalism tend to use simple and efficient food preservation methods, avoiding over-storage and taking a conscious approach to buying and consuming. This helps them maintain a tidy kitchen, reduce waste and maximize the utility of food.

Chapter 6

Minimalism in art: form of expression and social criticism

In the art world, minimalism has become a form of expression and a powerful tool for social criticism. Through simplicity and the reduction of visual elements, minimalist artists have managed to convey profound messages and provoke reflections in the viewer. In this chapter, we will explore how minimalism has left its mark on contemporary art, challenging traditional conventions and redefining the boundaries of artistic expression.

Minimalism in art finds its roots in earlier art movements, such as constructivism and abstract art. These movements laid the foundation for the minimalist approach, which sought the fundamental essence of form and color. Pioneers of minimalism such as Donald Judd, Dan Flavin and Agnes Martin, broke with established norms and explored the reduction of visual elements as a unique form of artistic expression.

Minimalist art is characterized by the simplification and reduction of visual elements to the essentials. He uses simple geometric shapes, clean lines, and neutral colors to create works of art that spark the viewer's attention. In addition, minimalism considers space and environment as integral elements of the work, creating installations that interact with the environment and generate an immersive experience.

For the minimalist, art has become a form of social criticism, questioning established norms and challenging concepts rooted in society. Through decontextualization and subversion, minimalist artists seek to undermine power structures and raise uncomfortable questions about social and political issues. By reducing the work to the essentials, the viewer is invited to an experience of contemplation and reflection, generating a dialogue on fundamental issues.

Art has also been used as a form of political statement. Minimalist artists challenge established standards of beauty and question rampant consumerism in contemporary society. Through their art, they criticize overproduction and the negative environmental impact of consumer society, promoting a more sustainable and conscious vision.

In short, minimalism in art has proven to be a powerful form of expression and an effective tool for social criticism. Through the simplification and reduction of visual elements, minimalist artists convey profound messages and challenge established norms. Whether through decontextualization, reflection or subversion, minimalism in art invites the viewer to an experience of contemplation and reflection, generating a dialogue on social, political and existential issues. In a world full of visual noise, minimalism invites us to return to the essentials and rethink our perceptions and beliefs.

Chapter 7

Impact on personal economy

As we have addressed above, minimalism is a lifestyle that has gained popularity in recent years due to its focus on simplifying and reducing the amount of material possessions. Although at first glance it may seem a concept related only to the personal sphere, minimalism also has a significant impact on the individual economy. In this chapter, we will explore how the adoption of minimalism can influence personal economics, both in terms of financial savings and in creating a more conscious and sustainable mindset in relation to consumption.

One of the main ways minimalisms affects the individual economy is through reducing spending and encouraging savings. By simplifying and minimizing material possessions, people who embrace minimalism tend to spend less money on purchasing unnecessary goods. This allows them to allocate their financial resources to things they consider more valuable, such as saving for emergencies, investing or finding meaningful experiences instead of accumulating objects.

Minimalism can also have a positive impact on eliminating debt. By reducing spending and purchasing non-essential items, people can allocate more resources to pay off their existing debts. By freeing oneself from financial burdens, new opportunities open for economic stability and independence.

Another important aspect of minimalism is the change of mentality towards consumption. Instead of constantly pursuing the acquisition of material goods, minimalism promotes a more conscious and reflective attitude about what is really needed and adds value to a person's life. This involves carefully evaluating purchases, considering their long-term impact, and prioritizing quality over quantity. By adopting this mindset, people can avoid impulse purchases and spend their money more deliberately, which leads to better financial balance and greater satisfaction with purchases made.

Minimalism is also closely related to sustainability and care for the environment. By reducing excessive consumption and waste of resources, it contributes to the preservation of the environment. In addition, the reuse, recycling and purchase of durable products are encouraged, which can have a positive impact on the individual economy and society in general.

Ultimately, minimalism goes beyond simply being a lifestyle trend, as it also has a significant impact on the individual economy. By adopting this approach, people can reduce their spending, save more money, eliminate debt, develop a conscious and sustainable mindset, and enjoy greater financial stability and greater satisfaction with their consumption choices, offering us the opportunity to live with less, but at the same time, get more in terms of quality of life and peace of mind.

Another aspect to consider is the way minimalists manage and manage their money. Managing money in a minimalist way implies knowing how to manage personal finances. Here are some key strategies to achieve this:

- Set your priorities: Identify your core financial values and goals. What is the most important thing for you in terms of money? It can be saving for retirement, traveling, owning a home, or anything else. By being clear about your priorities, you can consciously allocate your resources and avoid spending on things that don't bring you true value.

- Create a minimalist budget: Create a budget that reflects your basic needs and priorities. Eliminate superfluous expenses and focus on the essentials. This involves reducing spending on entertainment, clothing, gadgets and other non-essential objects. Be sure to put a portion of your income toward saving and the financial goals you've set for yourself.

- Avoid impulsive consumerism: What it is about is to buy consciously and reflectively. Before you make a purchase, ask yourself if you really need the item and if it adds value to your life. Give him time to reflect before acquiring anything, especially when it comes to large purchases. Consider the quality and durability of products rather than quantity.

- Eliminate debt and avoid new debt: Debt can be a financial and emotional burden. As a minimalist, it's important to free yourself from existing debts and avoid new ones as much as possible. Allocate a portion of your income to pay off your debts and use strategies such as the snowball method or the highest payment method to speed up the debt elimination process.

- Focus on experiences rather than possessions: Instead of spending money on material things, consider investing in meaningful experiences. You can allocate your resources to travel, spend quality time with loved ones, learn new skills, or participate in activities that you are passionate about. These experiences usually have a more lasting and significant impact on your life than the accumulation of objects.

- Practice financial sustainability: Like environmental sustainability, financial sustainability is important in minimalism. This involves living within your means, avoiding waste, and saving for the future. Prioritize quality over quantity and look for durable products instead of constantly buying cheap things that wear out quickly.

Remember that money management as a minimalist is about aligning your financial actions with your personal values and goals. Focus on what really matters and seek simplicity and efficiency in your financial decisions.

Chapter 8

Minimalism in the work environment

Minimalism is not limited only to the personal sphere; it can also be applied to the work environment. Being minimalist at work involves adopting a mindset and a simplified approach, eliminating excess distractions and prioritizing what's important. In this chapter, we'll explore how being minimalist at work can increase productivity, reduce stress, and improve job satisfaction.

A first step to being minimalist at work is to organize and simplify your workspace. Eliminate clutter and keep only the essentials on your desktop. Get rid of unnecessary papers, keep cables tidy and use an efficient storage system to keep your digital documents organized. A clean, tidy workspace can help you focus better and increase your productivity.

As a minimalist at work, it's critical to prioritize your tasks and projects. Identify which are the most important tasks and focus on them, avoiding dispersion and excessive multitasking. Use time management techniques, such as the Eisenhower matrix or Pomodoro technique, to organize and prioritize your activities. This will help you perform more effective work and avoid feeling overwhelmed by overwork.

In a work environment full of distractions, being minimalist means eliminating those that do not contribute to your productivity. Turn off unnecessary notifications on your phone or computer, set schedules for checking email and social media, and avoid falling into the endless cycle of unproductive meetings. By reducing distractions, you'll be able to focus on important tasks and complete them more efficiently.

Simplicity is key to being minimalist at work. Examine your processes and look for ways to simplify them. Identify repetitive or unnecessary tasks that can be eliminated or automated. Use efficient tools and software that save you time and effort. By simplifying processes, you can free up time to spend on more meaningful tasks and increase your overall productivity.

Being minimalist at work involves focusing on quality and results rather than the quantity of work done. Avoid the "do it all" mentality and instead prioritize delivering meaningful results. Focus on the tasks that generate the greatest impact and avoid work overload that doesn't add real value. By doing so, you'll be able to accomplish more with less effort and improve your job satisfaction.

It also involves seeking a healthy work-life balance. Avoid overwork and set clear limits for your time outside of working hours. By prioritizing your activities and simplifying your work approach, you can free up time and energy to enjoy other important areas of your life.

It should be recognized while relationships between co-workers can be affected by a person's minimalist approach. Below are some considerations on how labor relations can be influenced by minimalism:

- Focus on collaboration and teamwork: As a minimalist, you're likely to value simplicity and efficiency at work. This can lead to a more collaborative approach and a greater willingness to work as a team. You will value the optimization of resources and efforts, looking for ways to simplify processes and achieve shared goals.

- Less interest in distractions or superficial activities: If you're a minimalist, you may have less interest in the distractions or superficial activities that often arise in a work setting. You can choose to focus more on essential tasks and avoid engaging in gossip or unimportant conversations. This can lead to a relationship more focused on work and less on non-relevant personal aspects.

- Appreciation for the quality of relationships: Being minimalist, you can value the quality of relationships over quantity. You may prefer to have a few meaningful and authentic relationships at work rather than having many superficial connections. This could lead to a more selective approach to the relationships you want to develop and maintain with your coworkers.

- Clear and direct communication: As a minimalist, you're likely to like clear and direct communication. You may prefer to avoid ambiguity and unnecessarily complicated communication. This can help establish more efficient and effective working relationships, as expectations and messages are conveyed directly and bluntly.

- Respect for space and privacy: Minimalism can also imply respect for space and the privacy of others. You can be more conscious of not invading personal space or interfering with the privacy of your coworkers. This contributes to an atmosphere of mutual respect and promotes healthy working relationships.

It is important to note that each minimalist person is unique and may have different approaches and preferences in their working relationships. These are just a few possible general considerations, and relationships between co-workers are also influenced by other factors, such as personality, values, and organizational culture.

Chapter 9

Relationship with new technologies

In today's digital age, new technologies play a central role in our lives. For a minimalist, adopting a conscious and balanced stance towards new technologies is fundamental. In this chapter, we will explore how a minimalist can manage their relationship with new technologies, take advantage of their benefits and avoid the possible negative aspects.

A key aspect of minimalism in relation to new technologies is to use them intentionally and consciously. Instead of allowing technologies to dominate our lives, a minimalist sets clear boundary and commits to using them productively and meaningfully. This involves being selective about the apps and devices you use and avoiding overexposure and overuse.

Minimalism advocates simplifying our lives, even in relation to new technologies. This involves performing a digital detox regularly, removing unnecessary apps, unwanted subscriptions, and digital content that doesn't add value. By simplifying our digital environment, we reduce distraction and focus on what really matters.

New technologies can often be a source of distraction and can hinder our ability to concentrate. As a minimalist, it's important to be aware of how we spend our time and attention. Set limits on how much time you spend on social media, email, and other online activities. As support we could use time management techniques, such as the Pomodoro technique, to stay productive and protect your focus.[1]

A central approach to minimalism is to value quality over quantity. This also applies to new technologies. Instead of looking to have all the latest apps and devices, a minimalist prioritizes quality and functionality. This involves investing in technologies that improve our lives and bring us significant benefits, rather than simply following the latest trends.

In the digital age, privacy and security are crucial issues. As a minimalist, it's important to be aware of

[1] The Pomodoro technique is a time management method that suggests working in 25-minute intervals, without interruption or distractions, and adding 5-minute break times. Your goal is to set goals and improve productivity. Fountain: https://blog.hubspot.es/sales/tecnica-pomodoro.

how we protect our personal information and stay informed about the privacy practices of the platforms and apps we use. Take security measures, such as strong passwords and two-factor authentication, to protect your information and maintain peace of mind.

Minimalism reminds us of the importance of finding a healthy balance between technology and real life. It's critical to set clear boundaries and spend time on off-screen activities such as human contact, nature, and self-reflection. By doing so, we can enjoy a more balanced and meaningful life.

A minimalist uses new technologies consciously and sustainably. Here are some ways in which a minimalist can apply these principles in their relationship with technology:

- Conscious buying: It is important to carefully consider technology acquisitions and avoid falling into the trap of unbridled consumerism. Before making a purchase, evaluate whether you really need the device or app, and whether its acquisition will contribute to your well-being and minimalist lifestyle. In addition, a minimalist may choose to buy quality electronics that are durable and can be repaired, rather than falling into planned obsolescence.

- Sustainable use of electronic devices: You must strive to extend the useful life of your

electronic devices. Instead of switching pho-
nes or computers with each new version that
comes on the market, a minimalist uses their
devices until they really need to be replaced. In
addition, adopt proper maintenance practices,
such as regular cleaning of unnecessary files
and programs, and battery care to prolong the
life of devices.

- Digitization and reduction of paper consumption: An important aspect of minimalism is
  to reduce paper consumption and simplify
  life. A minimalist can take advantage of new
  technologies to digitize documents and reduce
  the need to print or accumulate paper. Using
  scanning and cloud storage applications allows
  documents to be accessed efficiently without
  the need to maintain physical files.

- Responsible energy consumption: We have at
  the same time to be aware of the energy consumption associated with the use of technologies. Turn off electronic devices when not in
  use, adjust display brightness settings to save
  power, and use smart plugs to reduce standby
  power consumption. In addition, a minimalist
  may consider using renewable energy sources
  to power their devices whenever possible.

- Responsible management of personal data: A minimalist values your privacy and the security of your personal data. It uses strong passwords, enables two-factor authentication, and informs itself about the privacy policies of the online apps and services you use. In addition, it minimizes the amount of personal information shared online and adopts digital security practices to protect your identity and avoid unnecessary risks.

By integrating awareness and sustainability into their relationship with new technologies, a minimalist can enjoy the benefits of technology responsibly and aligned with their minimalist values.

Chapter 10

Simplify your life and improve your physical health

In this chapter, we'll explore the impact of minimalism on our physical health and how simplifying our lives can contribute to overall well-being. As we delve into the world of minimalism, we'll discover how this approach can help us take better care of our bodies, improve our quality of life, and encourage a healthy lifestyle.

The minimalist lifestyle encourages us to get rid of clutter and unnecessary possessions, which reduces the stress and anxiety associated with maintenance and organization. A clear and tidy environment can promote relaxation and tranquility, contributing to better mental and physical health. Stress reduction has direct benefits on cardiovascular health, the immune system, and the endocrine system.

By having fewer possessions, we gain physical space in our homes and workplaces, allowing us to move more freely. A larger space makes it easier to do physical activities at home, such as yoga, strength exercises or even dancing, which encourages an active lifestyle. Freedom of movement can help prevent injury and improve flexibility and posture.

The minimalist philosophy invites us to also simplify our diet, focusing on quality food and avoiding the overabundance of options. Reducing processed foods and choosing fresh, nutritious foods can improve digestive health, the immune system, and metabolism. Mindfulness in food choices and consumption can help us maintain a healthy weight and foster a healthier relationship with food.

Simplifying our lives can allow us to devote more time and attention to our needs for rest and sleep. By reducing distractions and unnecessary stimuli before bed, we can improve the quality of our sleep.

Restful sleep has positive effects on physical health, such as strengthening the immune system, improving cognitive performance, and regulating hormones related to appetite and metabolism.

Minimalism simultaneously offers us a powerful perspective to improve our physical health by simplifying our lives. By reducing stress, increasing mobility, focusing on mindful eating, and prioritizing rest, we can experience greater vitality and overall well-being. Taking a minimalist approach can be a path to a healthier, more balanced life.

Minimalism can have a positive impact on our physical health in several ways. Here are some highlights:

- Physical space and cleanliness: With this we reduce the number of possessions and clutter in our environment. This allows us to have more physical space available in our homes, making cleaning and maintenance easier. A clean, tidy space can contribute to better air quality, reduce dust and allergen buildup, and create an overall healthier environment.

- Less stress and anxiety: Living surrounded by excess possessions can lead to stress and anxiety. Preoccupation with holding and organizing objects can be exhausting and consume our mental energy. By reducing the amount of stuff, we have, we can free ourselves from that burden and experience a sense of relief. Reducing stress and anxiety has a positive impact on our physical health, as chronic stress can contribute to a variety of health problems, including cardiovascular disease, sleep disorders, and digestive disorders.

- Greater ease of movement: By owning fewer objects, we become more flexible and mobile. This can have a direct impact on our physical health, as having fewer things to carry or move can reduce the risk of muscle or joint injuries. In addition, a minimalist home with less furniture and obstacles can also help prevent falls and accidents.

- Encouraging a healthy lifestyle: Minimalism promotes a more conscious and deliberate approach towards our daily choices and habits. By simplifying our lives, we can devote more time and energy to taking care of ourselves. This may include adopting a balanced diet, regular physical exercise, adequate rest and reducing harmful habits. By focusing on the essentials and eliminating distractions, we are better able to prioritize our health and well-being.

While minimalism can have physical health benefits, it's important to remember that it's not a silver bullet. Physical health is a result of multiple factors, including genetics, lifestyle, and other environmental factors. Minimalism can be a useful tool to encourage healthier living, but it's important to combine it with other healthy approaches and find the right balance for everyone.

Chapter 11

Connecting with nature

In this chapter, we will explore the relationship between minimalism and our connection to nature and animals. Minimalism is not only about simplifying our lives, but also about cultivating an ecological and ethical awareness towards the natural world around us. As we examine this relationship, we will discover how minimalism can help us better appreciate and protect nature and the living things that inhabit it.

The minimalist philosophy invites us to question our consumption patterns and reduce our material needs. By acquiring fewer material goods, we reduce our ecological footprint and decrease the extraction of natural resources. By opting for sustainable and ethically sourced products, we can promote production practices that are more respectful of the environment and animal rights.

By simplifying our lives, we can spend more time being outdoors, enjoying nature and connecting with it. This connection with nature helps us appreciate its beauty and understand our interdependence with the natural environment.

Minimalism encourages greater awareness of the ethical treatment of animals and urges us to reconsider our consumption choices related to animal products. By reducing or eliminating the consumption of animal products, we can contribute to the reduction of animal suffering and the decrease of the meat and dairy industry, which has a great environmental impact. It drives us to look for sustainable and animal-friendly alternatives, such as adopting a plant-based diet and choosing cruelty-free products.

By living with less and reducing our dependence on natural resources, we contribute to the conservation and preservation of ecosystems. It allows us to appreciate the beauty and importance of biodiversity, motivating us to support conservation initiatives and take action to protect the natural habitats of animals.

The connection with nature and animals and minimalism goes hand in hand, as both imply a change of mentality towards a more conscious and responsible life. By embracing minimalism, we can cultivate a greater appreciation for nature, promote sustainable and ethical consumption practices, and work towards the conservation and protection of animals and their environment. In doing so, we not only improve our own lives, but also contribute to a more balanced and harmonious world for all forms of life.

As a minimalist we must perceive nature with great appreciation and respect. We should see it as a refuge of beauty and serenity, a reminder of the simplicity and harmony it seeks to reflect in its own life.

The minimalist tends to value experiences in nature over material possessions. He enjoys spending time outdoors, whether it's hiking trails, admiring natural landscapes, or simply observing wildlife. The connection with nature is a source of inspiration and renewal for a minimalist.

At the same time, we must foster an attitude of conservation and care towards nature. By simplifying their life and reducing their consumption, a minimalist contributes to the preservation of natural resources and the reduction of their environmental impact. We can participate in actions such as recycling, reducing waste, choosing sustainable products and promoting environmentally friendly practices.

In short, a minimalist sees nature as a source of inspiration, peace, and connection. He values it as a reminder of the importance of living in harmony with the natural environment and seeks to protect and preserve its beauty for future generations.

Chapter 12

Finding the Inner Balance

In a modern world full of distractions and excesses, more and more people are feeling overwhelmed and discontented. In search of inner peace and balance, they have found refuge in an approach to living known as minimalism. Minimalism is much more than a simple visual aesthetic or decorating style. It is a lifestyle that seeks to eliminate excess and focus on the essentials. In this chapter, we will explore how minimalism can lead to inner peace and emotional balance.

Minimalism invites us to question our possessions and evaluate their true value in our lives. By freeing ourselves from the burden of excess material things, we can find a sense of lightness and simplicity that allows us to focus on what really matters. By simplifying our surroundings, we remove visual clutter and create a quiet space that gives us mental calm and clarity. By reducing the noise of our lives, we create space for introspection and reflection, allowing us to connect with ourselves on a deeper level.

The minimalist philosophy also extends beyond our material belongings and invites us to explore our relationship with our emotions and thoughts. Often, we carry a heavy emotional burden, holding on to past resentments, unfulfilled expectations, and future fears. Minimalism teaches us to practice emotional detachment, to let go of what no longer serves us, and to accept what we can't change. By freeing ourselves from these emotional burdens, we find a sense of peace and lightness, allowing us to live in the present and enjoy every moment.

It invites us to examine our relationships and focus on those that are truly meaningful. Often, we find ourselves immersed in social media and superficial connections that distract us from authentic and meaningful relationships. By simplifying our relationships and cultivating deeper, more genuine connections, we find a greater sense of belonging and emotional satisfaction. By surrounding ourselves with people who support and nurture us, we create an environment of love and support that contributes greatly to our inner peace.

It challenges us to find a healthy balance between our material needs and our spiritual needs. It encourages us to seek happiness and satisfaction in experiences and relationships rather than in the accumulation of material goods. By focusing on our personal growth, practicing gratitude, and connecting to something greater than ourselves, we find deep and lasting peace.

The spiritual atmosphere of a minimalist is characterized by simplicity, calmness and connection with the essential. Although minimalism is not necessarily tied to a specific religious practice, there can be a spiritual dimension to a minimalist's life that focuses on the search for meaning, the connection with oneself and with something greater than oneself.

The minimalist focuses on the following:

- Tidy physical space: They tend to have a clear and tidy physical environment. The elimination of clutter and excess possessions allows to create a calm and harmonious space, which contributes to inner peace and mental focus. An environment free of unnecessary visual distractions facilitates introspection and concentration on spiritual aspects.

- Meditation and mindfulness practices: The practice of meditation and mindfulness often goes hand in hand with minimalism. These practices help you to be present in the current moment, to develop a greater awareness of your thoughts and emotions, and to cultivate a deeper connection with yourself. Meditation can serve as a space for spiritual reflection and the search for inner peace.

- Valuing the intangible: They tend to value experiences and meaningful relationships more than material goods. Instead of seeking happiness in accumulating possessions, they focus on cultivating moments of joy, gratitude, and connection with others. This implies giving importance to the intangible, such as love, compassion, friendship and personal growth, aspects that can be considered spiritual.

- Connection with nature: They are often attracted to nature and find inspiration and serenity in it. Spending time outdoors, enjoying natural beauty, and connecting with the earth can be a way to nurture the spirit and find inner peace. Appreciation of nature can lead to a greater awareness of the interconnectedness of all things and foster an attitude of respect and care towards the environment.

- Search for meaning and purpose: It can also spark a search for meaning and purpose in life. By simplifying and eliminating the superfluous, space is opened to reflect on what really matters and what you want to focus energy and time on. This search can lead to the exploration of personal values, connection to spiritual or philosophical beliefs, and the development of a deeper purpose in life.

In general, the spiritual environment of a minimalist is characterized by an openness to introspection, connection with the essentials and the cultivation of inner peace. Each person can live minimalism differently and find their own way to nurture their spiritual life within this approach to life.

Chapter 13

Living Now with Less

In our modern society, where consumerism and the accumulation of material goods are considered the path to happiness, minimalism emerges as a philosophy of life that proposes a radically different approach. It invites us to simplify our lives, stripping ourselves of the unnecessary and focusing on the essential. In this chapter, we will explore how minimalism and the practice of living now can converge, and how this combination can lead to a more meaningful and fulfilling life.

Living in the now involves being fully present in the present moment, not allowing the past or the future to distract us. By practicing mindfulness and mindfulness, we can experience the fullness of each moment and find beauty and meaning in the simplest things. The now gives us the opportunity to appreciate life as it is, cultivate deeper relationships, and connect with our most authentic essence.

Living the now and minimalism are two approaches that complement each other perfectly. By embracing minimalism, we eliminate distractions and free up our mind and physical space, allowing us to be more present in the moment. At the same time, living in the now helps us appreciate and value what we have instead of constantly looking for more. Minimalism frees us from the "have" mentality to allow us to "be" fully in the present.

To incorporate minimalism and live the now into our daily lives, we can start by examining our material possessions and getting rid of what doesn't bring us value or joy. By simplifying our environment, we create a more orderly and tranquil physical space that helps us focus on the present. In addition, we can practice mindfulness and gratitude, paying attention to the smallest details of our daily lives and recognizing the blessings that surround us.

Minimalists tend to value the present and the "here and now." Minimalism is a lifestyle that focuses on simplifying and reducing excess in all areas, including material possessions, obligations, and distractions.

In doing so, they seek to focus on what is important to them and fully enjoy the present moment.

They recognize that too many possessions and commitments can lead to stress, anxiety, and a sense of lack of control over their lives. By minimizing the number of material things and commitments they have, they can free up time, space, and energy to devote to the things that really matter to them. This allows them to live more consciously and appreciate meaningful experiences and relationships in the present.

In addition, minimalism can also help reduce the focus on the past or future. By removing clutter and unnecessary distractions, they can be more present in the current moment, paying full attention to what they are doing, the people they interact with, and the experiences they are living.

However, it's important to note that minimalism doesn't involve completely denying the past or the future, but rather finding a healthy balance. Minimalists can value memories and lessons learned from the past, as well as plan and set goals for the future. However, they try to avoid clinging to the past or worrying excessively about the future, so that they can fully enjoy the present.

Tends to perceive the present time in a conscious and evaluative way. By simplifying their life and getting rid of unnecessary distractions, they can be more present in the current moment and make the most of it.

Instead of being constantly preoccupied with the past or the future, minimalists strive to live the "here and now." This involves paying mindful attention to your actions, thoughts, and emotions in the present moment, without getting carried away by rumination or constant anticipation.

By valuing present time, we can focus on meaningful experiences and authentic relationships. They seek to find joy and fulfillment in the little things in life, rather than relying exclusively on the accumulation of material possessions. This may involve enjoying simple moments, such as a conversation with a loved one, a nature walks, or a home-cooked meal.

In addition, they tend to give priority to activities that add value and meaning to them in the present. They can focus on personal development, pursuing passions and creative projects, caring for their physical and emotional well-being, and connecting with their environment and community.

In short, a minimalist perceives the present time as an opportunity to live consciously, appreciating what they have in the current moment, seeking meaningful experiences, and focusing on what really matters in their lives.

Capítulo 14

Time management

The fast pace of modern life, replete with endless tasks and overwhelming commitments, can leave us with the feeling that time is slipping through our fingers. During this maelstrom, minimalism has emerged as a revolutionary approach to simplifying our lives and finding meaningful balance. But what is the relationship between minimalism and time management?

In this chapter, we will explore how minimalism can become a powerful tool to manage our time more efficiently and consciously. As we unravel the fundamentals of both concepts, we'll discover how simplifying our lives and focusing on the essentials can help us free up valuable time for what really matters.

Throughout this chapter, we'll discover how minimalism and time management can complement each other to create a more balanced, meaningful, and purposeful life. Get ready to explore practical strategies, inspiring concepts, and thoughtful exercises that will help you embrace minimalism and make the most of your time on this exciting journey to a simpler, more fulfilling life.

A minimalist manages time consciously and focused on the essentials. Here are some strategies they typically use:

Set priorities: As minimalists we must identify the most important and meaningful activities and tasks for us. Set clear goals aligned with our values and focus our time and energy on achieving those goals. This involves making conscious decisions about how to use time and allocate it to activities that really matter.

Eliminate the unnecessary: Minimalists seek to get rid of unnecessary tasks and commitments that do not bring value or satisfaction. They regularly review their agendas and to-do lists, identifying those activities that they can eliminate, delegate or simplify. By doing so, they free up time for what is important in their lives.

Avoid multitasking: They tend to avoid multitasking and instead focus on one task at a time. They know that dividing their attention between various activities can result in lower efficiency and quality of work. By dedicating time and mindfulness to one task before moving on to the next, they can complete them more effectively and focused.

Set limits: They recognize the importance of setting limits on their time. This may involve saying "no" to commitments that don't align with your priorities, setting specific times for activities, and setting limits on your use of electronic devices and social media. By setting boundaries, they can protect their time and focus on what's most important to them.

Practice disconnecting: They understand the importance of disconnecting and taking time to rest and recharge. They can schedule moments of rest and relaxation in their day to day, as well as periods of digital disconnection. By taking time to take care of their well-being and renew their energy, they can stay focused and productive in their activities.

Practice mindfulness: They usually practice mindfulness and awareness in their daily activities. This involves being fully present in what they are doing, without getting carried away by distractions or worries. By being aware of the present moment, they can make the most of each activity and enjoy greater satisfaction in their experiences.

The minimalist learns to say "NO" consciously and deliberately. Saying "no" is a crucial skill for setting boundaries and protecting our time and energy. They recognize the importance of prioritizing their activities and commitments. By saying "no" to demands and requests that don't align with their priorities and values, they can free up time and energy to focus on what really matters.

Often, the minimalist tries to simplify and get rid of the unnecessary in all areas of life, including activities. By saying "no" to activities that don't bring significant value or distract us from our goals, we can free up time for what really matters.

Saying "no" allows us to set clear and healthy boundaries in our relationships and commitments. By learning to say "no" respectfully but firmly, we can avoid feeling overwhelmed or exhausted from taking on more than we can handle. Setting boundaries helps us take care of our physical and mental health.

Learning to say "no" can be challenging, as we often want to please others or are afraid of missing opportunities. However, minimalists recognize that saying "no" is an integral part of taking care of themselves and living a more authentic and balanced life. By consciously setting boundaries and saying "no," we can create an environment that supports our most important goals and values.

In short, minimalists manage their time consciously and focused on the essentials. They eliminate the unnecessary, set clear priorities, avoid multitasking, set boundaries, practice disconnection, and cultivate mindfulness. By adopting these practices, they can make the most of their time and live a more meaningful and balanced life.

Chapter 15

Our Choice

In this chapter we will explore the relationship between minimalism and our choice. At first glance, it might seem that minimalism limits our options by reducing the amount of stuff we have. However, as we delve deeper into this topic, we discover that minimalism can, in fact, expand our choice by allowing us to focus on what really matters and make more conscious choices.

Minimalism invites us to examine our material possessions and consider which ones are important to us. By freeing ourselves from the excess of unnecessary objects, we experience a sense of detachment and realize that we don't need so many things to be happy. This allows us to free up physical and mental space to make more conscious and meaningful decisions.

By adopting a minimalist lifestyle, we seek to simplify every aspect of our life. This implies reducing unnecessary commitments, eliminating tasks and activities that do not add value to us and focusing on the essentials. By simplifying our lives, we reduce the mental and emotional load, giving us greater choice by having more time and energy to invest in what really matters.

The minimalist philosophy invites us to divert our attention from the accumulation of material goods to the search for meaningful experiences. By reducing the importance of possessions, we realize that experiences and relationships are what truly enrich our lives. By choosing to focus on these experiences, we expand our options and open the door to greater satisfaction and fulfillment.

The minimalist lifestyle encourages us to question our choices and make more conscious choices in all aspects of our lives. By removing the noise and distraction of excess choices, we can better assess our needs and priorities. This allows us to make decisions aligned with our values and goals, rather than being carried away by external expectations. By exercising our choice more deliberately, we empower ourselves and create a more meaningful life.

Although it may seem paradoxical, minimalism can expand our choice by freeing us from the weight of material possessions and allowing us to focus on what really matters. By letting go of the unnecessary and seeking simplicity, we open space to make more conscious choices and enjoy meaningful experiences, reflect on our choices, and live according to our values and goals, leading to a more fulfilling and authentic life.

Minimalism makes us have power over our own lives. By adopting a minimalist lifestyle, a person makes conscious and deliberate decisions about what to own, how to spend their time and energy, and what experiences to pursue. It involves a focus on simplicity, clarity, and intentionality, which gives greater control and power over your life.

By reducing excess material possessions, you are freed from the emotional and mental burden associated with the accumulation and maintenance of unnecessary objects. This allows you to focus on what really matters and make decisions based on your own needs and values, rather than getting carried away by external expectations or societal pressures.

Moreover, by opting for meaningful experiences rather than accumulating material goods, the minimalist has the power to enrich their life in a deeper and more meaningful way. By directing your attention to relationships, experiences, and personal growth, you exercise your power of choice to live a fuller, more fulfilling life.

In short, minimalism empowers the individual by freeing them from the burden of excessive consumerism and allowing them to make conscious decisions aligned with their values. By simplifying and focusing their life on the essentials, the minimalist can live in a more authentic way and have greater control over their own destiny.

Chapter 16

Money management and finances

The minimalist philosophy can be applied to money management and personal finances, as it seeks to avoid excessive consumerism and foster a healthy relationship with money. In this chapter, we'll explore how minimalism can influence our financial decisions and help us achieve economic stability.

One of the fundamental principles of minimalism is to question our needs and desires. Instead of letting ourselves be carried away by the impulse to acquire more things, minimalism invites us to reflect on what we really need to live a full and satisfying life. By applying this mindset to our finances, we can reduce unnecessary expenses and allocate our resources to what we truly value.

Minimalism encourages us to be aware of how we spend our money. To achieve this, it is crucial to develop a detailed budget that reflects our priorities and financial goals. By setting clear boundaries and allocating our money deliberately, we can avoid waste and maximize the use of our resources. Conscious budgeting also helps us identify patterns of unnecessary spending and find ways to reduce them.

Debt can be a significant burden on our financial lives. Minimalism drives us to face and eliminate debts actively, avoiding the accumulation of interest and unnecessary financial burdens. By focusing on living with less, we can allocate a greater portion of our income to pay off debts and free ourselves from financial pressure. In addition, simplifying our finances, such as reducing the number of credit cards or bank accounts, helps us maintain better control over our resources.

It can also influence our investment decisions. Instead of looking for quick profits or following the latest trends, we can take a more conscious and long-term approach when investing our money. This involves carefully researching and selecting investments that are aligned with our values and financial goals. In addition, we can avoid the accumulation of unnecessary goods and spend on meaningful experiences rather than material possessions.

It also teaches us to value saving and planning. By reducing superfluous expenses, we can allocate a greater amount of our income to savings and the creation of an emergency fund. This gives us financial security and allows us to face unforeseen events without having to resort to debt. In addition, by taking a minimalist approach to our finances, we can free up resources for long-term investments.

A minimalist can organize their finances and invest their money consciously and aligned with their minimalist principles. Here are some steps to follow:

- Set priorities: Before starting to organize finances, a minimalist should reflect on their financial values and goals. This will help you determine what's important and set clear priorities.

- Create a minimalist budget: A budget is an essential tool to control expenses and direct money towards what really matters. A minimalist can create a minimalist budget, allocating funds only to essential needs and those things that really bring value and happiness to your life.

- Reduce unnecessary expenses: It is about eliminating the unnecessary, and that applies to expenses as well. You can review your expenses and eliminate those that do not add value or that are not consistent with our priorities. This may include reducing consumption of material goods, canceling unnecessary subscriptions, or renegotiating contracts for better rates.

- Saving deliberately: Saving is critical to long-term financial stability. Savings can be deliberately made by allocating a specific percentage of income to an emergency fund and short- and long-term financial goals. This ensures that the money goes to what is important and impulsive spending is avoided.

- Invest consciously: When investing, a minimalist can focus on options that are aligned with their values and goals. You can research and select ethical, sustainable or socially responsible investments. In addition, it encourages long-term investment, avoiding speculation and seeking the creation of wealth in a gradual and stable way.

- Avoid unnecessary indebtedness: It involves avoiding the accumulation of unnecessary debts. A minimalist can use the money he saves by cutting expenses to pay off existing debts and avoid taking on new debt as much as possible. This frees up financial resources to invest and achieve economic independence.

In conclusion, the relationship between minimalism and the organization of finance lies in the search for simplicity and intentionality in the management of money. Minimalism invites us to reevaluate our needs and desires, develop a conscious budget, reduce unnecessary expenses, avoid debts and save deliberately. In addition, when investing, a minimalist can select options aligned with their long-term values and goals. By adopting this minimalist approach, we can free ourselves from the pressure of consumerism.

Remember that everyone has their own interpretation of minimalism, so these recommendations can be tailored to individual needs and values. The most important thing is to seek a healthy relationship with money and use it as a tool to live a meaningful and fulfilling life.

Chapter 17

Simplifying Love and Conflict as a Couple

In this chapter, we will explore how minimalism can be applied as an effective tool for resolving conflicts in a relationship. Minimalism, as a lifestyle, promotes simplification and the elimination of the unnecessary, which can help us address disagreements and tensions in the relationship more effectively and harmoniously.

Minimalism teaches us to be clear and honest about our needs and wants. When facing conflict in the relationship, it is essential to express our feelings openly and sincerely. Avoiding the accumulation of negative emotions and communicating clearly helps prevent misunderstandings and find faster and more effective solutions.

Sometimes, conflicts in the couple can be complicated and overwhelming. Minimalism invites us to simplify and reduce the problem to its essence. By focusing on the fundamentals and avoiding the accumulation of unnecessary details, we can find solutions more easily and prevent the conflict from getting bigger.

It's not just about simplifying our physical belongings, but also about simplifying our minds and emotions. By practicing active listening, we strive to genuinely understand our partner's feelings and perspectives. This helps us establish more effective communication and find common ground to resolve conflict constructively.

Instead of focusing on winning an argument or being right, minimalism invites us to prioritize emotional connection with our partner. It is important to remember that we are in a team relationship and that the main goal is to maintain a loving and healthy connection. By adopting this mindset, we can find solutions that satisfy both parties and strengthen the couple bond.

Minimalism teaches us to let go of unnecessary emotional burdens, such as rancor and resentment. These feelings can hinder conflict resolution and damage the long-term relationship. By practicing forgiveness and compassion, we can free ourselves from negative emotions and focus on finding mutually beneficial solutions.

It drives us to look for practical and simple solutions. Instead of further complicating the conflict, we should seek alternatives that are feasible and realistic. By maintaining a focus on practical solutions, we can resolve disagreements more quickly and efficiently, thus preventing conflict from dragging on unnecessarily.

It teaches us to shed the unrealistic expectations we often accumulate in our relationships. By simplifying our expectations and focusing on the essentials, we can avoid unnecessary tensions and conflicts stemming from pressure to meet unrealistic standards.

In a relationship, we often carry unnecessary emotional burdens that can generate conflicts. Therefore, a minimalist philosophy of life urges us to free ourselves from emotional excess, such as resentment, resentment and ego. By letting go of these negative emotions, we can open space for understanding, forgiveness, and resolving conflicts more constructively.

The simplification of love involves clear and honest communication. Minimalism encourages us to express our needs and feelings directly and sincerely, avoiding misunderstandings and confusions that can trigger conflicts. By practicing open communication, we encourage mutual understanding and problem solving more efficiently.

Instead of looking for an excessive amount of time together or activities, minimalism invites us to prioritize quality in our interactions. By simplifying our schedule and focusing on meaningful moments of connection and mutual support, we can strengthen the relationship and reduce the likelihood of conflict caused by lack of time or attention.

Finally, it invites us to practice gratitude and appreciation in our relationships. By simplifying our lives and focusing on what really matters, we can cultivate an attitude of gratitude towards our partner and value the positive aspects of our relationship. This creates an environment of respect and love, which reduces the likelihood of conflict and fosters harmony.

The application of these principles in conflict resolution in a relationship can be extremely beneficial. By simplifying our expectations, communicating clearly and honestly, prioritizing the quality of our interactions, finding practical solutions, and cultivating gratitude, we can strengthen our relationship and create a space of lasting love and harmony.

Chapter 18

Simplify and Stand Out in the Academic Environment

In this chapter, we will explore how minimalism can be effectively applied in the academic setting to achieve outstanding success. Minimalism, as a lifestyle, encourages simplification and the elimination of the unnecessary, which can optimize our academic efforts, reduce stress and promote deeper and more meaningful learning.

Minimalism teaches us to clear clutter and create a clean and organized study space. By eliminating unnecessary distractions and maintaining an environment conducive to learning, we can increase our concentration and productivity, allowing us to excel in our academic tasks.

In academia, we often accumulate many books, notes, and materials. Minimalism drives us to simplify and reduce the number of belongings and materials to the essentials. By getting rid of the unnecessary, we achieve greater clarity and focus on our studies, facilitating access to relevant information.

In the academic setting, there are numerous opportunities to participate in extracurricular activities. However, minimalism encourages us to prioritize quality over quantity. By choosing activities that are meaningful and aligned with our academic interests and goals, we can maximize our time and energy, resulting in more enriching experiences.

It urges us to focus on deep and meaningful learning rather than seeking the superficial accumulation of knowledge. By carefully selecting the topics of study that we are passionate about and related to our goals, we can dive into them, understand them at a deeper level, and apply that knowledge effectively.

It teaches us to simplify our schedule and set clear priorities. This involves eliminating unnecessary activities and dedicating quality time to the most important academic tasks. By having a well-structured and balanced schedule, we can efficiently manage our time, minimize stress, and optimize our academic performance.

It invites us to practice digital disconnection and mindfulness in the academic environment. By limiting digital distractions, such as social media and electronic devices, and cultivating moments of mindfulness during study and classes, we can improve our concentration, information retention, and learning quality.

A minimalist student approaches study in a simplified and focused way. Here are some practices and strategies you could follow:

- Eliminate distractions: Create a study environment free of unnecessary distractions. This involves turning off electronic devices or putting them in silent mode, finding a quiet, tidy place to study, and avoiding any objects or activities that might divert attention.

- Simplify study space: Keep your study area clean and organized. This involves clearing clutter and keeping only the essentials needed for study, such as books, writing materials, and specific tools.

- Use digital study materials: Choose to use digital study materials instead of having a lot of books and physical notes. This reduces physical clutter and allows access to materials more conveniently and efficiently.

- Focus on quality over quantity: Instead of trying to study the entire syllabus superficially, a minimalist student focuses on the quality of learning. This involves carefully selecting the most relevant topics of study and devoting time and effort to understanding them in depth.

- Set clear goals: Set clear and realistic goals for your study. This involves identifying the specific objectives you want to achieve and focusing on them, avoiding the dispersion and accumulation of irrelevant tasks.

- Practice time management: Use time management techniques to maximize your productivity. This may include the Pomodoro technique, where you work in focused time intervals followed by short breaks, or careful planning of the study schedule to avoid procrastination and maintain a proper balance between study and rest.

- Taking breaks and taking care of wellness: A minimalist student understands the importance of regular breaks and taking care of mental and physical well-being. Adequate breaks are allowed during the study to recharge, practice relaxation activities or physical exercise, and maintain a healthy balance between study and other aspects of life.

This approach applied to the academic environment can transform a student's experience, allowing them to maximize their learning, reduce stress, and maintain a healthy balance in their academic life. By simplifying study space, eliminating unnecessary distractions, and focusing on the essentials, an environment conducive to concentration and productivity can be created.

In addition, by prioritizing quality over quantity, you move away from the mentality of accumulation of superficial knowledge and focus on understanding in depth the topics relevant to your academic and professional development. This not only encourages more meaningful learning, but also allows them to excel in their area of study.

Efficient time management and setting clear goals are fundamental practices for the minimalist student. By using time management techniques and setting realistic goals, they can optimize their productivity and avoid procrastination.

However, a minimalist student also recognizes the importance of taking care of their mental and physical well-being. You are allowed to take regular breaks, practice relaxation activities and maintain a proper balance between studying and other areas of your life. This helps them maintain a sustainable approach and enjoy a more balanced and rewarding academic experience.

In short, adopting the minimalist approach in the academic environment allows students to simplify and optimize their study experience. By eliminating the unnecessary, focusing on the essentials, and prioritizing quality, they can achieve deeper learning, reduce stress, and achieve outstanding success in their academic journey.

Chapter 19

Simplify Your Wellness: Take Care of Your Body and Health

In this chapter, we will explore how minimalist philosophy can positively influence our body and health care. Applied to the care of our body and health, minimalism offers us a perspective that allows us to make conscious decisions and create healthy and sustainable habits.

A minimalist approach helps us simplify our self-care routine. Instead of using a lot of products and treatments, we focus on those that are essential and beneficial for our body and skin. This allows us to save time, money and avoid exposure to unnecessary chemicals.

In the care of our body urges us to adopt a conscious and balanced diet. We focus on consuming fresh, natural and nutritious foods, avoiding excess processed and sugary foods. In addition, we seek to reduce food waste and choose to buy and consume only what is necessary.

A minimalist approach helps us develop a simple and effective exercise routine. Instead of chasing fads or expensive equipment, we focus on activities that we really enjoy and that suit our needs and preferences. This allows us to maintain a consistent exercise routine and enjoy the benefits for our physical and mental health.

It also invites us to disconnect and take care of our mental health. We give ourselves permission to have quiet and solitary moments, reducing constant exposure to technology and distractions. We practice relaxation techniques, such as meditation or mindfulness, to calm the mind and reduce stress.

Rest and sleep are fundamental to our health and well-being. Minimalism helps us prioritize adequate rest and create an environment conducive to restful sleep. We eliminate clutter in our bedroom, create a consistent sleep routine, and disconnect from electronic devices before bed.

Health is extremely important for a minimalist person. It is not only about reducing material possessions, but also about simplifying and improving all aspects of life, including health. Here are some reasons why health is valued by minimalist people:

Minimalists recognize that health is critical to overall well-being and quality of life. Good physical and mental health allows you to enjoy life to the fullest and perform daily activities with energy and vitality. By taking care of our health, we ensure we have the energy and well-being needed to devote ourselves to the things that really matter in life, such as meaningful relationships, hobbies, personal goals, and contribution to society.

What is ultimately about is seeking to reduce stress and anxiety. Physical and mental health is critical to achieving this goal. By taking care of our health, we decrease the risks of stress-related illnesses, improve our ability to handle daily challenges, and feel more balanced and calmer.

Minimalism also applies to self-care. By focusing on the essentials, we seek to simplify our care routines, opting for healthy and natural options. This helps us avoid over-products, saves time and money, and reduces exposure to unnecessary chemicals.

In conclusion, it can have a positive impact on the care of our body and health by encouraging simplicity and mindfulness in our daily actions. By taking a minimalist approach, we move away from the consumerist mentality and focus on the essentials, avoiding the excess of products and treatments that can be harmful to our body.

By simplifying our self-care routine, we free ourselves from the pressure of following the latest trends and focus on what really matters: nourishing and caring for our body in a natural and healthy way. This involves choosing quality and environmentally friendly products, but also limiting their quantity and using only what is necessary.

In addition, it invites us to be aware of our actions and decisions in relation to our health. By having fewer distractions and unnecessary commitments, we can devote more time and energy to taking care of our body and mind. This includes regular exercise, a balanced diet, adequate rest and emotional care.

By adopting a minimalist mindset in the care of our body and health, we find a balance between satisfying our needs and avoiding excess. We break free from rampant consumerism and focus on what really makes us feel good and healthy. It allows us to simplify and focus our lives on what really matters, thus promoting a comprehensive and conscious care of our body and health.

Chapter 20

A simplified retirement

In this final chapter, we will explore how the principles of minimalism can be effectively applied in retirement planning. Retirement is a period of life that requires careful financial and personal preparation, and minimalism can offer a unique perspective to simplify this process and pursue a more meaningful and fulfilling retirement.

A minimalist in retirement planning starts by reassessing your needs and priorities. It questions what is important for a full and meaningful life in retirement and seeks to simplify your expectations and desires by aligning them with your core values.

Minimalism is based on living with less and reducing excessive consumption. A minimalist in retirement planning looks for ways to reduce unnecessary expenses and save consciously. This involves assessing current expenses, eliminating the superfluous, and prioritizing saving to ensure a stable financial retirement.

Instead of complicated and risky investments, a minimalist in retirement planning looks for simplified, low-maintenance financial strategies. Look for investments that are safe, reliable and aligned with your long-term goals, avoiding the need for constant monitoring and minimizing associated stress.

A minimalist in retirement planning understands that happiness and satisfaction do not come from the accumulation of material goods, but from meaningful experiences and emotional connections. Look for ways to enjoy retirement through simple activities, such as enjoying time outdoors, cultivating creative hobbies, or engaging in volunteer activities.

Minimalism in retirement planning includes focusing on personal health and well-being. It seeks to maintain a healthy lifestyle through a balanced diet, regular physical exercise and mental health care. Understand that good health is essential to fully enjoy retirement.

A minimalist in retirement planning values interpersonal relationships and seeks to cultivate meaningful connections with family, friends, and the community. It recognizes the importance of maintaining and strengthening the social support network during retirement, which contributes to greater satisfaction and emotional well-being.

The minimalist philosophy can have several advantages at retirement age. Below are some of the advantages they may experience:

- Financial freedom: Promotes the reduction of consumption and unnecessary spending. By living with less and spending mindfully, minimalist retirees can accumulate significant savings and achieve financial freedom faster. This gives them greater flexibility and lifestyle choices in retirement.

- Less financial stress: By having less debt and superfluous expenses, minimalist retirees experience less financial stress. Planning and focusing on the essentials allows them to live within their means and avoid worries related to money. This contributes to a more relaxed and peaceful retirement.

- Simplified lifestyle: It involves living with fewer material possessions and focusing on what really matters. Minimalist retirees can free themselves from the burden of caring for and maintaining a large amount of material goods, allowing them to enjoy a simpler and less complicated lifestyle. This translates into less stress and more time and energy to devote to what they are truly passionate about.

- Greater flexibility and mobility: By living with fewer possessions and having fewer material ties, they can enjoy greater flexibility and mobility. They have the freedom to travel, move, or explore new experiences without the constraints of having to manage many belongings. This allows them to make the most of their time and resources during retirement.

- Focus on the meaningful: Minimalist retirees can focus on meaningful activities and relationships that bring them joy and fulfillment at this stage of life. They can spend more time with loved ones, participate in volunteer activities, develop hobbies, or explore new passions.

Overall, it can provide retirees with greater financial freedom, less stress, a simplified lifestyle, and a greater ability to focus on what's meaningful. By living with less and focusing on the essentials, minimalist retirees can enjoy a more satisfying, meaningful, and peaceful retirement.

Conclusion

Minimalism has emerged as a powerful antidote in our contemporary society, characterized by overabundance and complexity. Through the search for essence, simplification and liberation from the superfluous, minimalism offers us a path to a more meaningful, balanced and authentic life.

In this book, we have explored the various aspects of minimalism, from its influence on design and aesthetics to its impact on our daily lives, the environment and our quality of life. We've found that minimalism isn't just about reducing our material possessions, but also about clearing our mind and heart of distractions and unnecessary burdens.

By embracing minimalism, we free ourselves from the pressure of accumulation and excessive consumption. Instead of seeking happiness in ephemeral material possessions, we learn to value meaningful experiences, moments, and relationships. By simplifying our lives, we find room for personal growth, creativity, and well-being.

Minimalism also invites us to reflect on our impact on the environment and to take concrete steps to reduce our ecological footprint. By consuming consciously, avoiding waste and opting for sustainable products, we become agents of change that contribute to the preservation of our planet.

Ultimately, minimalism gives us the opportunity to live with greater intention and in tune with our deepest values. It challenges us to question the *status quo* and to design our lives according to our own authentic priorities and desires.

As I close this chapter, I invite each reader to reflect on their own path to minimalism. There is no single answer or foolproof formula. Each of us has the freedom to find our own balance and adapt the principles of minimalism to our individual lifestyle and circumstances.

By embracing minimalism, we embark on a journey of self-discovery, authenticity and well-being. We free ourselves from the chains of consumerism and move closer to a fuller, more meaningful life. As we move along this path, we can find deep satisfaction in simplicity and in the ability to appreciate the essential.

Let this book be a starting point for exploring and embracing the principles of minimalism in your own life. May it inspire you to take concrete actions and live according to your deepest values. May it help you discover beauty in simplicity and find true happiness in the essentials.

Printed in Great Britain
by Amazon